DRUNK AND CONFUSED

An Engineer's Approach To Sobriety

JEFFREY HOLLEY

Dedication

In loving memory of my dear grandfather, whose unwavering support and boundless wisdom continue to inspire my every endeavor. Your presence may be missed, but your memory and love remain eternally engraved in my heart. Thank you for instilling in me a passion for learning and personal growth. This book is dedicated to you as a tribute to the profound impact you had on my life and as a testament to the enduring legacy of your spirit.

With all my love,

Jeff Holley

Acknowledgment

I would like to extend my heartfelt gratitude and appreciation to the neuropsychological community, the Substance Abuse and Mental Health Services Administration (SAMSA), and the American Psychological Association (APA) for their invaluable contributions to the field of cognitive behavioral therapy (CBT) and addiction research.

To the dedicated researchers and scientists within the neuropsychological community, thank you for your commitment to understanding the complexities of addiction and for continuously expanding our knowledge of the neurobiological processes involved. Your groundbreaking studies and insightful findings have paved the way for advancements in therapeutic techniques, contributing to more effective and evidence-based treatment strategies.

I would also like to express my sincere appreciation to the APA for their continued support and promotion of excellence in psychological research and practice. Their commitment to fostering innovation, collaboration, and education has been instrumental in bringing about meaningful change in the field of addiction treatment. The APA's dedication to disseminating knowledge and serving as a platform for scientific exchange has greatly enriched both the scientific community and the lives of individuals struggling with addiction.

Furthermore, special acknowledgment goes to the countless patients and participants who have graciously shared their experiences and journey toward recovery. Your bravery and openness have shaped the research landscape and continue to inspire and motivate professionals in their quest to provide effective interventions and support.

Lastly, I would like to express my deep gratitude to my colleagues, mentors, and friends, who have provided invaluable guidance, encouragement, and feedback throughout the writing process. Your insights and passion for the field have been an endless source of inspiration.

In conclusion, this book stands as a testament to the collaborative efforts of the neuropsychological community and all contributing organizations that have paved the way for a better understanding of cognitive-behavioral processes and addiction. I hope that this work will contribute to further advancements in treatment and ultimately enhance the lives of those struggling with addiction.

Thank you all for your untiring dedication and support.

Sincerely,

Jeff Holley

Contents

About the Author

Jeff Holley, an accomplished Pharmaceutical Process Engineer, has a deep-rooted passion for engineering and a steadfast commitment to the field. Born in Oxford, Ohio, he earned his Bachelor of Science degree in Chemical Engineering from the University of Cincinnati. Jeff's commitment to education persists as he pursues a Master's degree in Engineering Management at Johns Hopkins University.

Throughout his career, Jeff has held significant roles in the pharmaceutical and engineering sectors. While employed as a Senior Process Engineer at AstraZeneca, he played a crucial role in developing and integrating production processes for the launch of the AstraZeneca vaccine from the United States. Jeff has also supported the development and launch of several life-saving medicines and medical devices at various companies.

Before his pharmaceutical career, Jeff served as an Ammunition Technician in the United States Marine Corps from 2006 to 2010, earning multiple Service Medals. He remains an active member of the Black Sheep Veterans Association and the Habitat for Humanity - volunteering in Northern Kentucky and Cincinnati, Ohio.

He is a member of prestigious professional organizations, including the Golden Key International Honour Society and the National Society of Leadership and Success. Jeff was also recognized by Marquis Who's Who® and received an Industry Leader's Award in 2023.

Jeff is an advocate for addiction awareness and mental health. He hopes that the research and treatment of psychological afflictions continue and that the importance of doing so remains a priority.

Outside of his professional life, Jeff finds joy in spending time with his wife, Katelyn Holley, and their five children. He delights in cooking, cherishing moments with his children, and enjoying the company of his two dogs, Bella and Louie.

Jeff Holley's outstanding career, dedication to his field, and devotion to his family set him apart as a remarkable individual. His diverse experiences and expertise continue to contribute significantly to the pharmaceutical industry and his community.

Preface

In writing this book, I aim to share my deeply personal journey of overcoming immense obstacles - the struggles that shaped me, the battles that pushed me to my limits, and the victories that transformed my life. It is both a story of pain and a story of triumph, one that delves into the profound impact of childhood and adult experiences on our development and mental well-being.

As I reflect on my early years, it becomes evident that the seeds of anxiety and depression were sown during my formative moments. Each chapter of my life unfolded with its own set of challenges that gradually shaped my perspective and perception of the world around me. The threads of my experiences have woven together into a tapestry of emotional turmoil, leading me down a treacherous path.

Amidst the turmoil, I found myself grappling with an addiction to alcohol - a desperate attempt to numb the pain and escape the clutches of my own mind. It became clear that my struggle with addiction was an extension of the deep-seated traumas I had endured. But beneath the darkness that overshadowed my life, there remained a glimmer of hope, a profound desire to break free from the chains that bound me.

This book is not solely a memoir of my struggles but also a testament to the strength of the human spirit and the power of resilience. It delves into the depths of addiction and the complexities of mental ailments, shedding light on the intricate web that connects them. It aims to challenge the stigmas surrounding addiction and mental health, emphasizing that they are battles fought by countless individuals.

As I embarked on my journey to recovery, I encountered a myriad of therapeutic and psychological methods that paved the way for my transformation. From traditional therapy to mindfulness practices, cognitive-behavioral techniques, and the support of those close to me, the path to healing presented itself through various avenues. Within the pages of this book, I lay bare the tools and insights that aided my recovery, hopeful that they might help others navigate their paths toward healing.

It is essential to acknowledge that no journey to recovery is without setbacks and moments of doubt. I am incredibly grateful for the unwavering support of my loved ones who stood by me, even during my darkest moments. Their compassion and belief in my capacity to overcome served as a constant reminder that I was not alone in this battle. As you read this book, I invite you to join me on an intimate exploration of triumph, vulnerability, and growth. Within these pages, you will find the stories that shaped me, the strategies that empowered me, and the insights that allowed me to transcend the clutches of addiction and reclaim my life.

May this book serve as a beacon of hope for those who find themselves grappling with similar struggles. Let it remind us all that within the depths of our pain, there lies the potential for transformation and the possibility of finding solace in the arms of recovery.

With heartfelt sincerity,

Jeff Holley

"No man is free who is not master of himself."

-Epictetus.

Chapter 1: The Hunt

"Life is warfare and a journey far from home."

-Marcus Aurelius.

I could have started this book a million different ways. How do you choose an origin or any moment of significance to represent your focal point? No idea. There are far too many variables, potential root causes, ideas, theories, or whatever bouncing around my mind to pick. Nevertheless, the sentiment remains the same - sharing my story with the hope that maybe someone out there will benefit from it. When I hear other people's stories, I always seem to resonate with some portion of them, not all, but there are always similarities. It's in those similarities that I seemingly find a little comfort in knowing that there are people just like me, dealing with issues just like mine, who want to have their lives back in their control, powered by their conscious thoughts and decisions. It's uplifting for me, personally, at least.

I originally began writing down my life story in chronological order as a therapeutic exercise. I was on a hunt for the cause of my discomfort in sobriety; I was combing through my life trying to piece together what could be the reason, or reasons, that caused me to feel this innate discontent. This feeling was with me all the time, regardless of time, location, surroundings, planet, or galaxy. I just felt unease, subtle but persistent. An expanding field of isolation and separation from what appeared to be "normal society". But what is normal society? I have no idea. I didn't grow up normal, my path through life thus far hasn't been normal, my personality isn't normal, my trauma isn't normal, and my emotions aren't normal. At least, that's what I tell myself. However, as time goes on, frankly, I don't really give a shit what's normal. I just want to feel OK being OK. I want to feel peace, steadiness, security, and contentment.

Getting back to the hunt. There are several large portions of my childhood and adolescence that I simply cannot remember. It's just not accessible. Not because I was high or drunk during those times, but because my mind chose to shade those areas so I don't see them anymore. Dissociative amnesia, apparently. For what reason exactly? Who knows, you could draw out of a hat and find a thousand reasons. Regardless, these gaps in my history sparked a curiosity, and along with this curiosity was an immense desire to simply figure my problems out, per se.

With these anticipations, I thought I should step through what I do remember to create some sort of timeline, and maybe that would help determine what's linked. Then, within my internal investigation, I could potentially find and pull out the rotten, aching tooth that haunts my daily life. It was a genuine, organic idea that I thought would help me eventually identify the source of pain. We all know when something hurts. If you get kicked in the shin, you're going to know your shin hurts. But what about when your mind hurts? What do you do when the source of the pain isn't something tangible or physical? Finding the source of that pain is a mysterious venture, a wicked and unfortunate one that some of us experience. It's a sick game at times, but like any game, with practice, you get better. With this game, however, if you don't show up to practice, even on your days off, holidays, and sick days, the consequences could be fatal. It's not a game I chose to play, I didn't volunteer or ask for this shit, but nevertheless, I'm the quarterback, the driver, the captain, the sniper.

On a quest for epiphany, I started writing out my life from as early as I could remember until the present. I reviewed the piece several times, occasionally remembering events here and there and adding them in their respective places. Who knows what's relevant at this point. My life began to have a storyline. It all began to flow from one stage to the next. I could see how feelings and emotions propagated and how they influenced my behavior, decisions, and, subsequently, my entire mentality. I couldn't fill in all the gaps, but with my newfound internal understanding, I at least had material to work with. I wasn't empty-handed anymore, begging the universe for answers. I had datapoints I could analyze.

My hunt became fruitful. I was finding lingering sources of anger, resentment, fear, and sadness. Events from my childhood I now recognized were traumatic and far from my current understanding of "normal". Links were appearing, and these links formed the chain of my life - they couldn't be broken. But the weak links need fixing before the entire chain snaps, so that's what I set out to do. With the realization that there are no ways in which I can change anything that's ever happened, I must accept things as they are now and use my own aching mind to clever up the ideas to ensure the links I build from here going forward, are stronger and stronger each time.

We aren't born with addictions - we find them. We may be born more predisposed to obsessive or addictive behaviors, genetically speaking, or born into environments that affirm certain lifestyles. But the addiction itself forms from our unwavering need to subdue the pain, discomfort, anguish, and emptiness we experience consistently. That's how mine formed, at least. I look at addiction as a compelling and overwhelming desire to aid a pesterous ailment and to relieve persistent pain. Not all addictions form as a result of escaping pain or as a co-occurring disorder, but in my case, I believe it did. Regardless, the characteristics of the addiction itself remain the same. This aid and relief, albeit euphoric and rewarding, brings along with it a slew of unique ailments. However, these ailments are different, newer, and not as solidified as problematic as the original issue the addiction was treating. Our minds look toward the original pain we experienced with an obsessive desire to remove it from our lives, with the willingness to accept new pain in its place. So long as the original issue is gone, I'm good. So I thought.

It's important to note that considering this definition of addiction and viewing it from this perspective as opposed to a selfish pleasure-seeking compulsion, we can now look toward addicts of all types in a different light. Yes, the "solution" addicts/alcoholics find through their vices does become habitual, ritualistic, and progressive. Hence the need to abstain and find sobriety and so on. But originally speaking, the addict himself/herself is really just a person suffering. They/we found a way to ease the troublesome mental turmoil that distracts us and makes daily living a bitch sometimes. Why wouldn't we use this medicine?

In a very exaggerated example, say someone walked up to you and snapped your femur. That's going to hurt a lot and for a very long time if left untreated. Say, magically, Vicodin started raining from the sky, and one landed in your mouth. You swallow the 60mph pill, naturally, and soon, that tremendously painful, debilitating broken femur starts to feel a little better. You can think clearer now about how to get to a hospital before you most certainly die. Noticing the rewarding effects of Vicodin and its ability to return you to normal, you take more. Now, the pain is almost gone completely. You take a break from crawling towards the hospital to sigh in pure relief. "Thank God, I feel so much better now. I just want this to go away," you say to yourself. But, unfortunately, the Vicodin starts wearing off, and that pain is creeping back in, if not accelerating back in. Better go grab those Vicodin rain drops before you can't even crawl anymore. You don't want your friends, family, and coworkers to see you crawling on the ground with an obviously broken leg, do you? Hell no, that would be traumatically humiliating. Scoop up some rain drops and move on like normal. So the cycle begins: thought–craving–use.

With every revolution of the cycle, its borders grow thicker and harder to break. Getting out of that cycle grows increasingly difficult, especially with a broken leg. And before you know it, you're trapped.

The cycle has become your way of life now - it has to be it's the only way you can survive. Unless you can find a way to drill through the ever-thickening walls of this vicious beast, you're going to have to play along and learn to live your new lifestyle. Fast-forward 10+ years, how thick do you think the walls of the cycle have become? According to Hebbian Theory, pretty thick; the repeated and persistent stimulation of the post-synaptic cells associated with these behaviors has now made this cycle almost reflexive, and natural even. Rewind 10+ years; someone just broke your femur, and you know if you get to a hospital, they can fix it, and you can return to your life after some healing and physical therapy. But what about a situation where you don't know the source of the pain? What do you even treat? Do you even need treatment, or is this normal? Well, if this is normal, then normal sucks a lot.

To that end, why do other people's 'normal' seem better than mine? Am I missing something here, or just off a little? These personal comparisons snowball over time into an emotional avalanche. Without a way to center yourself, create connections with others, and express vulnerability, you create a protective shell that not only hides the seemingly 'abnormal' psychological traits you burden but presents your public persona. The version of you that you want to be seen by others. Personality management at its best.

Hard work though. Doing that every day, constantly filtering your speech, pre-generating responses, anticipating questions, and essentially rehearsing your day - each day - to ensure you're viewed appropriately and not perceived as being associated with the mental ailments you suffer from. That takes energy, motivation, will-power, and lots and lots of practice. However, will-power is like a muscle, and like any muscle, they eventually get tired and need to recuperate.

It's an exhausting feat and not a pleasant existence, really. I want my 'normal' to be like these other happy people's 'normal'. I work hard, I'm a good person, and I deserve that too. How do I get that? And gradually, the delving into drugs and alcohol is born. Instant relief and effortless moments caress your aching mind and tease you with happiness. It's a place you don't want to leave; it's the feelings you want but can't find on your own; it's the life you've worked for and the relaxation you deserve. You're forced to live in the present, and you don't even want to speculate about the future or anything to do with responsibility. You're right here and right now. Able to touch the things around you, smell, taste, and see. It's an uninhibited version of you.

But it's not real, and it's not sustainable. Living through a decade of alcoholism, I can vouch for the unfortunate return of reality each day and the need to address your responsibilities. That's the only way to get another ticket back into peaceful oblivion. However, the return of reality brings with it the requirement to face your fears and do things that may make you nervous, scared, or uncertain. Ironically, if instead of spending your free time with your face in a bottle to get relief, you spent it practicing therapeutic exercises and behaviors, those fearful activities wouldn't be all that bad. Over time, they may not even bother you at all. And at that point, there's no need to seek relief as the pressure has been lifted. That seems like a better alternative to active addiction.

Unfortunately, in my case, I had no idea where to even start. What do I even address? I couldn't define my "problem" mainly because it seemed like a holistic issue. It seemed like everything was wrong with me - the way I walked, talked, dressed, and behaved, my sense of humor, social skills, professional capacity, and intelligence, you name it. I thought it was wrong. My protective shell seemed like it was made out of steel by this point. I didn't want anyone to see who I really was; for that matter, I didn't even know who I was. Had I not matured enough, did I miss something? How are these other people seemingly all together, and I'm in pieces?

My internal questioning fueled a curiosity to find answers, a desire to obtain peace, and a yearning for a happier existence. I knew it was possible. I just needed to take the first step, even if it was a small one. I needed to approach my situation rationally and realistically if I wanted my efforts to be truly effective. I needed to address not only the things lingering from my past but my current afflictions as well: anxiety, depression, and alcoholism. It seemed like a daunting task when looking at it as a whole. But the good thing is not all of it gets addressed at once; not everything gets fixed right away with results overnight. I had to learn to be patient with myself, learn to accept myself as I was, and find a way to be happy in the present – not when everything is "fixed", but right then. It's a waste of life to wish your time away, and it's a futile exercise as there will always be challenges in life. Therefore, accept yourself as you are, knowing that you have things you're working on and improving, and keep moving forward a step at a time.

Chapter 2: Brain vs Mind

"I remained too much inside my head and ended up losing my mind."

-Edgar Allan Poe.

Before diving into my story, I think it's important to have a fundamental knowledge of our own neurological anatomy and physiology. If you already have that knowledge, then just consider this a refresher. There is quite a bit of information here, but it is important to be cognizant of our mental processes and where they come from.

We experience our feelings, urges, desires, repulsions, love & hate, pleasure & pain in a realm of consciousness within which we live – from the aggregation of chemical and electrical signals throughout our brain. Neural networks that have formed throughout our lives from good and bad experiences, learned responses, and presuppositions guide our thought processes, influence our behaviors, and produce our emotions. It's fascinating, at least to me, how we have this consciousness, this life, and yet we can trace it back to our own physiology (to the best of our knowledge). Our mind allows us to learn from the past, secure the present, and prepare for the future.

The human brain is a complex organ responsible for numerous functions, including processing information, controlling bodily functions, and generating thoughts and emotions. Understanding how the brain works can provide insights into various aspects of human behavior and mental processes, particularly addiction.

At the core of brain function are neurons, specialized cells that transmit electrical signals. These signals travel through the brain via neurotransmitters, chemical messengers that allow communication between neurons. Different neurotransmitters play a role in regulating mood, cognition, and overall brain function.

The brain's intricate network allows for the formation of thoughts and emotions. Thoughts are the result of neural activity in specific areas of the brain, while emotions are influenced by neurotransmitter activity and neural pathways related to mood regulation. These pathways grow and strengthen based on how much we reinforce them.

Neurotransmitters such as serotonin, dopamine, and norepinephrine play crucial roles in regulating mood. Imbalances in these neurotransmitters can contribute to mood disorders like depression or anxiety.

Furthermore, our thoughts can shape our experiences and behaviors. Neuroplasticity is a concept that refers to the brain's ability to change its structure and function based on experiences or thought reinforcement. This means that our conscious thoughts have the power to rewire neural connections over time, thus changing our own subconscious thinking.

Understanding how the human brain works provides valuable insights into mental health conditions, cognitive processes, and overall well-being. Ongoing research continues to unravel its complexities while shedding light on potential treatments for neurological disorders or ways to optimize cognitive function.

Our brain, as complex and intriguing as it is, creates our world based on experiences, feelings, events, anticipations, and even self-fulfilling prophecies. Our conscious acts as a filter, in and out, of the world and everything around us, which subsequently generates the reality in which we experience life. However, our subconscious plays a huge role in this as well.

Understanding the difference between the conscious and subconscious mind is crucial in gaining control over our thoughts and behaviors. The conscious mind refers to our awareness of thoughts, feelings, and actions that we actively engage in. It is responsible for logical thinking, decision-making, and problem-solving.

On the other hand, the subconscious mind operates beneath our conscious awareness. It holds a vast amount of information and influences our thoughts, beliefs, emotions, and behaviors without us realizing it. It is like a powerful database that stores memories, habits, and automatic responses.

While we have direct control over our conscious thoughts and behaviors, the subconscious mind plays a significant role in shaping them. Our subconscious beliefs and programming can impact how we perceive ourselves and others, as well as influence our habits and reactions to certain situations. Our subconscious houses the reflex for craving addictive substances or behaviors. It has learned, through prolonged reinforcement, that under certain circumstances, we must resort to the addictive substance or behavior as a solution to whatever the issue may be.

By understanding this distinction between the conscious and subconscious mind, we can begin to gain more control over our thoughts and behaviors. Through self-awareness techniques such as mindfulness and reflection practices, we can observe our thoughts objectively without judgment. This allows us to identify any negative or limiting beliefs stored in the subconscious that may be hindering personal growth or causing unwanted behavior patterns.

Once aware of these patterns or beliefs, we can actively work on reprogramming the subconscious through techniques like cognitive behavioral therapy (CBT), thought reframing, or visualization exercises. By consciously choosing empowering thoughts and beliefs while consistently reinforcing them at a deeper level through repetition or visualization, we can gradually reshape our subconscious programming. This reshaping of the brain is done through the concept of neuroplasticity. Overtime, we can change the neural networks we inherently use and, subsequently, the neurotransmitter activity and their associated levels in our brain. More on this later.

Different neurotransmitters play different roles in regulating emotions, reward, pleasure, pain, and moods. Prolonged substance abuse, or engaging in addictive behaviors, alters the levels of different neurotransmitters and pushes them outside of their normal range. The longer the substance abuse or addictive behavior continues, the more the brain adjusts these levels to a new "normal" to account for the substance/activity.

Listed below are some of the key neurotransmitters affected by substance abuse or addictive behaviors:

1. Acetylcholine (ACh): ACh is involved in various brain functions, including muscle contraction, learning, memory, and attention.

2. Serotonin: Serotonin regulates mood, appetite, and sleep. It also plays a role in emotional processing and is involved in the pathophysiology of depression and anxiety disorders.

3. Dopamine: Dopamine is associated with reward, motivation, movement, and pleasure. It plays a crucial role in the brain's reward and pleasure system and is linked to addiction, motivation, and certain mental health conditions.

4. Gamma-aminobutyric acid (GABA): GABA is the main inhibitory neurotransmitter in the brain. It helps regulate anxiety, stress response, and overall excitability of the nervous system.

5. Glutamate: Glutamate is the primary excitatory neurotransmitter in the brain. It is involved in memory formation, learning, and synaptic plasticity. However, excessive glutamate can lead to excitotoxicity, which can damage neurons.

6. Norepinephrine (noradrenaline): Norepinephrine is involved in arousal, attention, stress response, and mood regulation. It helps regulate heart rate and blood pressure.

7. Endorphins: Endorphins are neurotransmitters that act as natural painkillers and are associated with feelings of pleasure and well-being. They are released during activities such as exercise and laughter.

These neurotransmitters work together in complex ways to maintain the proper functioning of the brain and control various physiological and cognitive processes. Imbalances or dysregulation of these neurotransmitters can contribute to the development of neurological and psychiatric disorders. When you throw alcohol in the mix for a prolonged period of time, you change the normal levels of several neurotransmitters, which leads to withdrawal when alcohol use is suddenly stopped.

By diving deeper into how the brain works, through its regions, and the different signaling performed by various neurotransmitters, we can see on a more granular level how we ultimately experience happiness, sadness, etc. Emotional experiences are subjective, of course, and there is no way to necessarily quantify an emotion – meaning we can't say at "X" level of Dopamine a person will experience reward. It's different for each person, as is addiction and as is recovering from that addiction. What's important here is knowing that our thoughts, cravings, and urges are the result of this brain activity. It has been a learned response over time that has been persistently reinforced. Thus making it stronger and more subconscious over time. This same method can be used for good, however, when we approach recovering from this addiction in a neurological way.

Chapter 3: Developing You

"You have power over your mind – not outside events. Realize this, and you will find strength."

-Marcus Aurelius.

Life's experiences play a significant role in shaping who we are as people, as unique individuals incapable of being duplicated. They shape our beliefs, values, attitudes, and perspectives. Through the stages of childhood, adolescence, and the many phases of adulthood, we are consistently absorbing information, analyzing it, and using it. This isn't always a conscious process, however. Our minds can adapt and develop subconsciously, without our awareness of it, through gradual exposure or distinctive life events. This holds true for the formation of addiction and alcoholism as well.

Life experiences influence us in several ways, including – but not limited to – the following:

- ➢ Personal growth
- ➢ Shaping Identity
- ➢ Emotional Development
- ➢ Empathy and Understanding

➢ Decision-making

➢ Values and Beliefs

When talking about addiction and alcoholism, especially in the context of a co-occurring disorder such as anxiety or depression, I think it is critical to understand how we develop, as well as the cognitive areas that are shaped through our experiences. Zooming out from the different neurotransmitters and regions of the brain, we can now look at who we are as individuals – our moods, reactions, beliefs, spirituality, sense of humor, fears, etc. These aspects are the result of what we've learned over time and what we've experienced, and this is different for every person.

Our cognitive development is a gradual and successive process – we build off of previous experiences to prepare us for the next. Our brains gather information from events in our lives to store for use later when we experience a similar event. It's truly a survival instinct that allows us to respond to events appropriately for the best outcome. When our minds identify a successful response to a situation or event, they will retain the physical and emotional response and utilize it in the future. If we feel rewarded by an action, we are more likely to continue that action. However, if an action causes us pain, we would tend to avoid that action.

If, for example, every time you saw the color red, someone punched you in the face, what do you think your response to seeing the color red would be? After a few times of being punched, I'm sure the next time, you would probably try to block your face or even run away. You may experience a rush of adrenaline, fear, or anxiety about seeing red again. You'll begin to create an emotional response to the color red, such as anger or even sadness. Your emotions towards the color red continue to solidify as time goes on, and these emotions formulate your subconscious beliefs about the color red. These beliefs are automatic, a reflex response to the color red. Your new beliefs then lead to new behaviors about colors in general and the overall avoidance of seeing the color red.

The brain's way of retaining emotional and physical responses to external or internal triggers and events ultimately sets the groundwork for who we are. Our emotions and attitudes towards certain stimuli influence the development of our values and beliefs over time. This subsequently aids in the formation of our individual identity and self-image as we progress through later stages of childhood and adolescence.

Our emotional response and memory of events in our lives influence our self-image as well. The way we interpret and react to different situations shapes how we perceive ourselves and our abilities. When we respond positively to events, such as overcoming challenges or achieving goals, it boosts our self-esteem and self-confidence. This reinforces a positive self-image, as we see ourselves as capable and competent individuals. Conversely, if we respond negatively, such as experiencing failure or setbacks, it can lead to a negative self-image. We may doubt our capabilities, feel inadequate, or perceive ourselves as failures. This can dent our self-esteem and make it harder to view ourselves in a positive light.

Our self-image is also influenced by the meaning we attach to events. If we interpret a situation as a personal failure rather than a temporary setback, it can further impact our self-image in a negative way. On the other hand, if we interpret challenges as opportunities for growth and view setbacks as learning experiences, it can contribute to a more positive self-image.

People who experience traumatic events in their childhood, such as neglect, abuse, molestation, etc., are impacted psychologically in a way that alters their self-image. Some may feel they lack value or are less important than others. Children who are molested often find themselves attributing their self-worth to their bodies. These types of emotional alterations also play a key role in how we identify effective solutions to problems in our lives and effective responses to external and internal triggers and events.

The development of our self-image, how we perceive ourselves in the world, and our self-identity begin forming in early childhood as we become cognitively aware of the world around us. This development continues into and throughout adulthood as we continue to build upon the information we've gained thus far in our lives. Our early years have a profound impact on our thinking processes as adults. Understanding this fundamental concept can help in your journey to self-awareness and sobriety. Let's look at how childhood experiences play a crucial role in the shaping and developing of your adult mind:

1. Formation of beliefs and values: Childhood experiences, whether positive or negative, shape your beliefs and values. The environment you grew up in, the relationships you had with family and friends, and the experiences you encountered all contribute to your belief system, which continues to influence your thinking and decision-making in adulthood.

2. Attachment and relationships: The quality of your early attachments and relationships with primary caregivers can impact your ability to form healthy

relationships in adulthood. A secure attachment can lay the foundation for trusting, fulfilling relationships, whereas experiences of neglect or abuse can lead to difficulties in forming and maintaining relationships later in life.

3. Emotional development: Childhood experiences significantly impact emotional development. Positive experiences, such as feeling loved, supported, and encouraged, contribute to the development of emotional intelligence, empathy, and resilience. Conversely, negative experiences, such as trauma or neglect, can lead to emotional challenges and difficulty regulating emotions in adulthood.

4. Cognitive development: Childhood experiences play a critical role in cognitive development, including the development of problem-solving skills, critical thinking abilities, and language acquisition. The early years are a crucial period for brain development, and the stimulation and experiences provided during this time lay the foundation for cognitive growth in adulthood.

5. Self-concept and identity: Childhood experiences contribute to the formation of self-concept and identity. The way you were perceived and treated by others, along with the opportunities and limitations you experienced while growing up,

shape your sense of self and the beliefs you hold about who you are. This self-concept influences your self-esteem, self-efficacy, and overall well-being in adulthood.

Everyone will experience negative events at some point in their lives. The magnitude of how negative it's interpreted to be is subjective, as some people may be more affected by a specific situation than others. However, some experiences are traumatic to an individual, with lasting effects on the person's psyche. By definition, a traumatic event is a deeply disturbing or distressing experience. However, trauma isn't always a singular event. It can be the culmination of smaller negative experiences over time – whether it be from verbally demeaning comments, intense emotional disturbances, or long-term relationship difficulties.

Let's look at how trauma can have a significant impact on the psychological development of children and their self-image:

1. Emotional Development: Traumatic experiences can lead to emotional dysregulation, making it difficult for children to appropriately manage and express their emotions. They may experience increased levels of anxiety, fear, guilt, shame, and low self-esteem.

2. Cognitive Development: Trauma can disrupt cognitive development, affecting a child's ability to think, concentrate, problem-solve, and reason. It may also impact their memory and attention span, making learning and academic achievement more challenging.

3. Social Development: Trauma can interfere with the formation of healthy attachments and relationships. Children may struggle with trust, have difficulties forming peer connections, and exhibit social withdrawal or aggressive behaviors. They may also have trouble understanding and responding to social cues, which can impact their self-image.

4. Self-Concept and Self-Esteem: Trauma can distort a child's self-perception and negatively impact their self-esteem. They may develop a negative self-image, feeling unworthy, unlovable, or responsible for the traumatic event. This can affect their confidence, self-worth, and overall sense of identity.

5. Behavioral Changes: Trauma may lead to behavioral changes, such as aggression, withdrawal, hyperactivity, or difficulties with impulse control. These behavioral responses can also influence a child's self-image, as they may

internalize negative labels from themselves or others.

Understanding some fundamentals of how we develop has helped me process a lot of difficult thoughts and feelings that I've held onto for years. Having just the basic knowledge of our cognitive development, albeit a very complex process, helps as a guideline. As I reflect on my life thus far and rewind as far back to the beginning as I can, I'm able to see how some of my thought patterns may have developed over the years. The most important part of this is being able to ask myself if this thought pattern is rational or irrational. Am I processing information reasonably, or is this skewed based on some previous experiences of mine? Asking myself meaningful questions like this and allowing myself the opportunity to work through my thought process has been a tremendously effective tool for me in maintaining sobriety.

Since we've gone through some about how we develop as individuals, let's look a little at how alcohol addiction can develop. Before getting into it, the development of an addiction is a unique process based on the individual and a variety of circumstances. There is no one-size-fits-all description. As we covered, we can succumb to an addiction as the result of evading pain or as the result of prolonged use/exposure. So, we'll use my case as an example to avoid any generalizations.

Before my alcohol use became an active addiction, my mental health was in a pretty bad place. I was struggling with intense anxieties, both generalized and social. Naturally, depression came along to make matters worse. Due to my circumstances at the time, I was also going through some big life changes, some expected and some unexpected. Overall, the handful of years leading up to what I would consider the beginning of my addiction were riddled with personal, professional, and social challenges. As much as I wanted to convince myself that I could handle it all, I was actually falling apart.

Alcohol use was always a part of the social encounters I would have – I was used to it being almost expected when meeting up with friends, going out to eat, or doing anything purely social. I hadn't realized that, in my case in particular, I was also masking very low self-esteem, social anxiety, and envious tendencies while I drank. Having a co-occurring disorder to alcoholism makes things quite challenging. Even before addiction was an issue, anxiety and depression were becoming crippling. So intense that some days I couldn't leave the house, I would miss work or class at the time, miss family functions, etc. I would close all my blinds and literally hide from the outside world – I didn't have it in me to face my responsibilities or even talk to another person.

These personal issues I was enduring were a recipe for seeking relief. In addition to my mental health challenges, I also have a genetic predisposition for addictive behaviors. I get a positive neurological response from alcohol – therefore, when I drink, my brain sends reward signals in the form of Dopamine, making me crave more and consume it more frequently. As we covered above, my brain retains the physical and emotional response to events for use in the future, and my brain retains the positive response I got from drinking.

Having a pre-existing anxiety disorder and/or depression can contribute to the development of alcohol use disorder in several ways. Listed below are some common contributing factors:

1. Self-Medication: People with anxiety and depression may turn to alcohol as a way to self-medicate and temporarily alleviate their symptoms. Alcohol can provide a temporary escape from emotional pain and distress, making individuals feel calmer or more relaxed in the short term.

2. Increased Vulnerability: Anxiety and depression can make an individual more vulnerable to alcoholism. The emotional distress caused by these mental health conditions can weaken a person's ability to cope with stress and make healthy decisions. This vulnerability can lead to alcohol misuse or dependence.

3. Dual Diagnosis: Many individuals with anxiety and depression have a dual diagnosis of alcohol use disorder. The coexistence of both mental health conditions requires comprehensive treatment addressing both issues simultaneously. If one condition is ignored, the risk of relapse is higher.

4. Cycle of Dependency: Regular alcohol use can create a cycle of dependency, where individuals rely on alcohol to cope with their anxiety and depression. However, alcohol is a depressant, and excessive consumption can worsen symptoms, leading to a vicious cycle of worsening mental health and increased alcohol use.

5. Social Isolation: Anxiety and depression can contribute to social isolation and difficulties in interpersonal relationships. Alcohol can sometimes be used as a social lubricant and a means to connect with others. However, this reliance on alcohol to socialize can potentially

lead to unhealthy patterns of alcohol consumption and dependency.

It goes without saying that everyone's experience is unique, and not everyone with anxiety and depression will develop alcoholism. However, the presence of anxiety and depression can increase the risk of developing alcohol-related problems. What I should have done during my time of implosion was get professional help. As we all know, that's easier said than done.

If we turn my mental health prior to my active addiction into a basic equation, it's pretty obvious what it would equal. Anxiety + Depression + Overwhelming Stress + Personal, Professional, & Academic Pressures + Genetic Predisposition for Addiction + Frequent Alcohol Consumption = ? Yeah, pretty simple question. Let's look a little at this genetic predisposition topic regarding addiction.

Genetic predisposition refers to the increased likelihood of an individual developing a particular trait or condition based on their specific genetic makeup. When it comes to addiction, scientific research has shown that genetics can play a role in increasing the risk of developing substance abuse disorders.

Multiple genes are thought to contribute to this genetic predisposition for addiction, and research suggests that variations in certain genes can make individuals more susceptible or more resistant to developing addictive behaviors. These genes are involved in various processes within the brain, such as reward, pleasure, and the regulation of neurotransmitters. For example, variations in genes that code for dopamine receptors or transporters can affect how the brain responds to substances like drugs or alcohol. As we have seen, dopamine is a neurotransmitter associated with reward and motivation, and these genetic variations can influence an individual's sensitivity or response to dopamine, potentially increasing the risk of addictive behaviors.

Genetic predisposition is not a guarantee of addiction. Environmental factors, such as upbringing, social influences, and personal experiences, also play significant roles in the development of addiction. Therefore, genetic predisposition should be considered as just one factor among many in understanding addiction susceptibility. It's worth mentioning that understanding the genetic basis of addiction can have important implications for the prevention, treatment, and intervention strategies for substance abuse disorders.

Chapter 4: Part 1 – From Birth to Bullets

"We suffer more often in imagination than in reality."

-Seneca.

In the pages that follow, I've done what I can to condense my experience into a consumable, readable, and understandable format. I've reduced my life thus far into the next three chapters of this book, from as early as I can remember to the present. The events and situations included are ones that I believe have distinctive implications on the development of my psyche and, ultimately, the person I've become. The intent of the story that follows is for you to understand me on a more personal level, with the hope that somewhere within my life, you're able to find similarities and potentially gain something valuable.

My story begins in Oxford, OH. A small college town in the middle of nowhere and home of Miami University. It's a nice town with a surprising underbelly of recreational substances, gambling, guns, drug dealing, and lots and lots of alcohol. If you get to know the right (or wrong) people, you can get involved in that type of lifestyle, disturbingly young if you wanted to. However, on the flip side of that coin, there's a wealth of opportunity for young students to grow, learn, and expand their knowledge and skill set in preparation for their future careers. Miami is home to tremendous academic opportunities and fosters a healthy community on a stunningly beautiful campus.

It's truly two separate worlds, residing in parallel, uninfected by the other. Oil and water flowing in stream. Which flow you're absorbed by largely is up to you. Many people, including myself, find themselves at the juncture of Yin and Yang. Troubled by choice, fueled with potential and motivation yet afflicted by uninhibited curiosity and temptation. The middle ground is dangerous – it's not easy living both of those lives. If you're not careful and meticulous about your time spent on the dark side, it may just swallow you up. Disintegrating a wonderful mind and heart into a silhouette of what remains. I've known quite a few who haven't left the dark side, and unfortunately, the longer you're there, the harder it is to leave. Although I've also known quite a few who have excelled in their careers and personal lives to impressive heights, inspiring heights really, that lived in the same tiny town as me. How can that be when people with the same opportunities and resources available to them go in starkly different directions? There are too many variables to confirm any reason; interesting to think about, though.

Some people there go through their younger lives without any knowledge of the cohabiting universe that exists all around them - oblivious to the hardships of those less fortunate and the rougher lifestyles some live, either by choice or force. It's paradoxical. Nevertheless, I remained in the middle ground, semi-experiencing life through two lenses, unable to pretend the other doesn't exist and unable to fully engage in either.

I grew up with a sense of independence and self-reliance that was uncommon for someone my age. While other children had their parents hovering over them, guiding their every step, I navigated the world mostly on my own. It wasn't always easy, but it taught me valuable life lessons that shaped who I am today. I think it was through this independence that I grew my love of learning and my insatiable sense of curiosity. This independence also presented me with unique challenges along the way, socially and mentally.

My earliest memories begin with my life in a small townhouse when I was roughly four years old. Growing up, it was just my mom, my older brother, and me for the majority of the time. My mom had some fleeting relationships speckled throughout, but she was ultimately tasked with the burden of raising both my brother and me on her own. As a single parent, she had to work a lot to make ends meet and provide for us - she never received any considerable child support from either my brother's dad or my dad.

Throughout my life, and up until his passing in July 2018, my dad would only be present in brief, sporadic periods before disappearing again for years to come. My dad was a very intelligent man and an incredible musician. Music was something both my dad and I enjoyed, and that was a bonding point for us. He had taught me the basics of piano and drums as a kid, and I ended up playing the drums in the school band all through middle school. What I didn't know about my dad until I was a young adult was his struggle with addiction and that of his siblings and family as well. He struggled with Heroin addiction for the better part of 30 years, in and out of methadone clinics, until his liver couldn't take it anymore.

As kids, my brother and I fought perpetually. He is three years older than me and a lot bigger than I am, which didn't bode well for me whenever we fought. We had these innate, holistic differences that caused our personalities to clash. We just looked at life differently and were interested in different things. He was big into sports and football, and I was more on the sciencey, want-to-learn-everything side. We all know that brothers fight, but the frequency and severity of our fights were notable. The underlying tension and disdain for one another lasted our whole childhood. I learned to adapt to the dynamic the two of us had to prevent and avoid scenarios that I felt would anger him. This started the fire within me to eventually stand up for myself, against anyone, anything, any organization, or whatever, in a fierce way - a way that was hell-bent on proving it.

I can remember a handful of our fights where I was truly terrified - mom would be at work, and my brother would beat me up, either stomping my head onto the couch or trying to remove my bedroom door to get to me. I was defenseless and unprotected. Other times, he didn't like what I said or did and would sucker-punch me in the face. There was an essence of hatred involved, which I believe stemmed from our differences. We were like this for the majority of our childhood. I had to learn to dodge conflict with him, identify potential moods or behaviors that were linked to him getting aggressive, and essentially bite my cheek on many things I felt like saying in fear of his response. This internalization only amplified my anger and my resentment.

When I was 4 and 5, my mom had this boyfriend whom I currently despise. He was a strict, mean, cocky SOB who thought he was God's gift. He definitely wasn't, and looking back, he was just another piece of trash. He thought knowing how to fist fight was irrationally important, so while my mom was working, he would make my brother and I fist fight each other in the living room in front of him. This experience was both distressing and bewildering. It left a lasting impact on my young mind as I struggled to comprehend why such behavior was deemed important. I recall my brother saying, "Just keep going." It was a stark reminder of the turbulent environment I found myself in and the unsettling dynamics within our household.

This experience, in particular, has left indelible scars for many reasons and, in my opinion, was the seed for some of the behavioral traits to stem from as I grew up. Now, my mother never endorsed, supported, or even saw these events happen. But they did nonetheless.

The SOB wasn't in our lives for too long, and shortly thereafter, we moved to an apartment just down the street. We lived in this apartment for only about a year, although it was an eventful year. There were two boys in the neighborhood that didn't like my brother very much at the time, and they made sure we knew it. Almost every day for quite some time, the two kids would try to beat my brother up right as we got off the bus. It was nerve-wracking as we approached our stop, knowing what was about to happen and hoping they would just leave us alone. We would get off the bus, and before it could even pull away, the kids came after my brother. Screaming for help, I remember the bus just driving off. I would try to help my brother, but as I was much smaller and younger, I wasn't very useful. After the initial fighting, the two boys would taunt us and throw things at us the rest of our walk home. I don't recall exactly how long this routine lasted, but at the time, it felt like forever.

I distinctly remember the blend of emotions I was experiencing: a raw mixture of helplessness, sympathy, fear, and rage. I never understood why the bus driver, seeing me crying as I walked off the bus and in full knowledge of what these kids were about to do to us, did nothing to help and simply drove away amidst the violence just feet away from the vehicle. This was thought-provoking at the time, albeit confusing, but it prompted internal questions that drove developmental responses. Were we not important enough to protect? What was different about us than other children? Why is this only happening to us? Seeing other kids playing and laughing on the bus as we prepared to fight our way home was a catalyst for personal comparisons and value-seeking. It's as early as this that I can remember the first feelings of inferiority and separation. Within roughly a year of living there, we ended up having to move to a different townhouse across town. One of those kids had thrown a brick through our kitchen window, and following our complaint, the landlord asked us to move, as the other party had been long-time renters of his. Some resolution that was!

The new townhouse would be where we lived for the remainder of our time in Oxford. It was suitable for the three of us, with the exception of the train tracks that ran just some 50 feet from us. We got accustomed to the rumbling and the incredibly loud whistles over time. My brother and I were latch-key kids growing up, so we came and went as needed and looked after ourselves a lot. Starting around the 2nd grade, I would ride my bike to and from school, come home and do my homework, and then go outside until dinner time. I spent a significant amount of time outdoors, exploring the streets of Oxford and venturing wherever my curiosity led me. As a child, I enjoyed the freedom of unrestricted exploration.

I spent most of my time as a young kid either exploring the city of Oxford or acquiring knowledge. I wasn't big on TV or video games; I was fixated on knowing as much as possible about as many things as possible. I figured out that people became impressed (on occasion) when I would talk about things or know certain things that would seemingly be over my head. This made me feel special and was a source of positive emotion for me. Being on my own a lot, I learned to be resourceful and adapt to various situations. Whether it was figuring out how to fix a broken bike, learning electrical wiring how mechanical devices worked, or even finding my way home when I got lost, I became adept at problem-solving. These experiences instilled in me a sense of resilience and determination that has been with me through many challenges in life.

Life was decent in our new townhouse. We were close to the city park, close to the uptown area, and close to some of the stores Oxford had at the time. I met some new friends in the neighborhood, too, which was nice. Life was sort of typical during this period, mixed with your expected ups and downs. However, as time went on, my mental struggles continued. I had a lot of self-doubt at this point in my childhood. I didn't have a lot of self-esteem, and it led me to question myself and my actions. Not really knowing how to express these emotions or the ability to even articulate them, they compounded over time. Left unaddressed, the negative thoughts were able to run rampant. I didn't know how to rationalize with myself at that age; not many kids do, as far as I know. I was impacted by overwhelming internal questions about my own value as a person, questioning if I was even important to those in my family and why I felt so lonely. I was too young to process thoughts of this magnitude. I remember phases where I would cry at night after going to bed, not really knowing why. I just remember feeling so lost, confused, and alone. I began to feel isolated and different from everyone. I seemingly had no value to the world, and that feeling became a belief.

I began to wonder how I could be viewed as valuable, important, and useful. What can I do to feel equal to everyone else? Growing up without feeling important or cherished made me crave validation from others. I yearned for someone to recognize my worth and show me the affection that seemed so unreachable. These thoughts festered as I took inventory of things I was good at, things that made me special and unique. This remained a consistent frame of mind for time to come.

My mom ended up taking me to counseling when I was around 9 or 10. I don't recall much about it or for how long I went. I can only remember the beginning of one session, and the rest is blank. As far as I can tell, it wasn't an effective approach to resolving what I was dealing with, and I don't really think I said much to the guy. I believe it was around this time that I began to live with the expectation of being looked down upon and not included in the general populous. At this age, I could see differences between my family and others and the difference in socioeconomic status. I wasn't able to simply overlook these things, as, in reality, those things don't matter, but to me at that time, it suited my depressive perspective. My mental response was interesting and ambivalent. I felt feelings of sadness regarding my perceived differences, yet also defensive and assertive about who I was and what I believed in. I was confident on one hand and foolish to believe that on the other. I embodied this mentality; I didn't know what else to do. I believed I was considered less than general society and that there was something wrong with me. So, I adapted. Yes, I was sad, but no, I wasn't giving up. I found defense in this arena through witty sarcasm, jokes, and insults, honestly.

As this thought process solidified, so did the belief that I had to hide who I really was. Prevent the public from knowing I'm just a maladjusted kid from a small family who's been disregarded and discarded from society as I knew it. Gradually, I was turning into your typical jokester and outspoken rule-breaker. This became my identity – juvenile delinquency coupled with intelligence and an insatiable desire to learn.

As I transitioned into middle school, I brought with me my attitude and newfound identity. I quickly became the class clown. It was an ironic role because I was a smart kid and found it easy to get good grades, so it seemed paradoxical to be the trouble maker. But this was all a front. I'm not cocky, I'm not a jerk, I'm not mean. It's all a cover. One that I would shed every day on my way home.

Teachers and principals were constantly confronted with the conflicting aspects of my personality - they recognized the untapped potential within me that I failed to acknowledge. Yet, they also had to address my mischievous behavior. Some teachers treated me like nothing more than a pestilence, while others were more patient.

During my seventh-grade year, I found myself spending a significant amount of time in in-school suspension. It was a challenging period for me as I struggled to find my place within the school community. I wanted so badly to be accepted by others. I wanted people to like me because if they liked me, then maybe I could like myself.

As I entered high school, my focus shifted towards cultivating new friendships and being romantically involved with girls. I was turning into a hopeless romantic with a rough side and lots of mental baggage. Aside from that, my high school career was speckled with skipping class, several arrests, drugs, alcohol, and partying.

I used to work as a cook in a restaurant in uptown Oxford, where most of my coworkers were college students. Naturally, I started spending time with them outside of work and getting into things they were doing. Life quickly transformed into a constant party, and I found myself becoming enslaved by the enticing atmosphere it offered.

As the days turned into nights, and the nights blurred into hazy memories, I found comfort in the temporary escape that drugs and alcohol offered. The party scene became my refuge from the suffocating weight of my internal struggles.

In those moments, I felt free. The numbness that washed over me drowned out the whispers of self-doubt and sadness that plagued my mind. It was a world where all my worries evaporated, replaced by a false sense of euphoria. I felt a sense of belonging, acceptance, admiration, and confidence. I could shed my self-doubt and step into a version of myself that I had always longed to be. The acceptance and understanding that radiated from those around me allowed me to finally embrace my quirks and idiosyncrasies without fear of judgment.

As high school progressed, the party scene became a constant in my life. It seemed like every weekend, there was a new party to attend, and I never wanted to miss out. Balancing school, work, and my social life became increasingly challenging, but somehow, I managed to keep up with my academic responsibilities.

My ability to maintain good grades despite my erratic attendance was a mystery even to me. I would often skip classes, only to find myself miraculously catching up on missed assignments and acing exams. However, as time went on, I began questioning the sustainability of this lifestyle. The constant cycle of school, work, and partying started taking its toll on me physically and mentally. My energy levels were constantly depleted, and I found it harder to concentrate.

Little did I know that this newfound resolution to my loneliness and depression was merely an illusion. The more I indulged in this unrestrained lifestyle, the more it consumed me. Over time, the parties became less about socialization and more about chasing an unreachable, substance-induced persona. What once seemed like a remedy soon transformed into chains that bound me to a never-ending cycle of self-destruction.

While those moments temporarily saved me from my internal struggles, they merely masked the deeper issues. The reliance on substances and the constant pursuit of external validation couldn't fill the void within me. It was a lesson I would only understand in the years to come.

Looking back, I see this phase of my life as a quest for connection, self-acceptance, and belonging. It was a journey through which I sought to escape the painful memories and emotions that lingered and continue my self-discovery.

During the summer before my senior year, two Army recruiters knocked at my door. They painted a vivid picture of life in the army, its adventures, and the opportunities it held. It all sounded thrilling, a world I had never considered before. The military was a realm I hadn't explored, a path I hadn't even glanced at.

As I looked more into it, the thought of becoming a Marine enticed me. It was something I could do directly out of high school and could potentially be a career. I graduated from high school a semester early on Friday, January 6th, 2006, and was on a plane—my first ever plane ride—to boot camp on January 8th, 2006, at the age of 17.

My time in the Marines was an experience impossible to forget. For the most part, I loved it. The organization, structure, discipline, and ability to do things at a global level gave me a sense of pride. Every day was structured, with strict routines and expectations that left no room for laziness or complacency.

The Marines were huge for me. I learned a lot about a lot and it gave me the discipline, focus, and guidance to become a self-sufficient young adult.

I slowed way down on the drinking while in the service; I just didn't feel the same need to do it. I was mentally preoccupied with everything the military required, which clouded my desire most of the time. Granted, I would have a couple of beers a few nights a week, but rarely anything beyond socially acceptable amounts.

I grew up very fast in the Marines, to a fault in some aspects. I got romantically involved with another female marine while I was stationed in California, despite overwhelming objections. I thought I found a long-term relationship and partner, someone I could eventually start a family with. However, I was too naive to see the red flags practically slapping me in the face. My longing to feel loved and fill the void created by years of disconnection and loneliness was finally going to be completed. We ended up getting married when I was 19, just a few months before I had to leave for deployment. My wife was pregnant with our son at this time, and he was born in January 2009 while I was overseas in Kuwait.

After my deployment, my time in the Marines was coming to an end. Towards the end of my contract, I had about 30 days of paid leave left, and I decided to use that time to move my family back to Cincinnati. I had big plans in mind: I wanted to create a stable life for us, build a family, pursue my dream of getting a chemical engineering degree, and start a promising career. It finally seemed like everything was falling into place.

Chapter 5: Part 2 – Engineering and Ecstasy

"Temptation can sway even the purest mind to sin, and the denialist to claim that tomorrow will bring change. However, the irrefutable truth is – tomorrow, my friend, never comes."

-Jason Worthley.

My life back in Cincinnati started pretty well. We had rented a townhouse and settled in relatively seamlessly. I had spent a few months before the move preparing everything logistically and financially. I was to begin college only a month after getting moved in and situated, and I needed to have a school set up for my stepdaughter at the time. My son was only 11 months old when we moved back to Cincinnati, and my wife wasn't working or doing school, so she was able to watch him during the day.

Being back in my home city, I immediately wanted to get together with old friends, assuming everything would pick up where it left off. I felt like I was back from a very, very long trip. However, as I reconnected with friends from my past and people in my hometown, I couldn't help but notice the stark contrast between our lives. Some had settled into stable careers, while others seemed content with their carefree lifestyles. It made me question my path and where I fit into this complex web of experiences.

Towards the end of my military career, I felt comfortable with the people I was around. I wasn't shy about who I was, and I was more at ease with expressing myself. I didn't feel like there was anything wrong with my life as it was, and the people I was surrounded by were all in similar places in life. It was like we all began at the same time – we had similar things outside of the military to talk about: kids, families, houses, etc. Honestly, things felt pretty in place and secure before leaving the military.

The more I socialized with old friends back home and hung out with them, the more curiosity consumed me. I really didn't have much in common with where they were in life and didn't have much to relate to. It felt like there was an invisible barrier separating us - a divide created by the different paths we had chosen. Attending college reinforced these thoughts. Being older than most of the traditional students, I found it challenging to make friends and be comfortable. I began to feel out of place, even around those I grew up with. As I observed the way people effortlessly navigated through conversations and chatted with new acquaintances, I constantly found myself questioning - how does everyone seem to know things I don't and understand themselves better than me? What am I missing, and what's wrong with me? Why do I feel so lost, out of touch, and different than the rest of the world? Why does everyone else seem to have it all figured out while I am left feeling confused and inadequate?

Looking through the lens of my mind, people became mysterious. The more distant I felt from them, the more I felt there was something wrong with me. It seemed as though they possessed a secret knowledge that dodged me, an understanding of themselves and the world that I couldn't grasp. This constant comparison only served to deepen my feelings of isolation and disconnect from the rest of the world.

As time went on, the weight of these thoughts became unbearable, taking a toll on my mental and emotional well-being. Each day, I carried the burden of self-doubt, wondering what was wrong with me that prevented me from fitting in or understanding life like others did. It felt as though I was drowning in a sea of insecurities, desperately searching for a way to feel at ease again.

To make matters worse, my home life offered no solace or support. Instead of finding comfort within my family, I felt like an outsider there, too. My wife and I were gradually growing apart, and our fundamental differences were becoming more and more visible. Our values and interests diverged so greatly that it seemed we were more distant with each passing day. I was growing in a very different direction than she was.

With each new day, the differences between her and I seemed to magnify, creating an ever-widening gap between us. Our interests, values, and even our ways of thinking clashed incessantly. It became increasingly clear that we were incompatible in most aspects of life. At the time, I was so consumed by my internal struggles, engineering school, kids, and finances that I couldn't truly process the emotions or the truth about my situation. I couldn't accept the reality I was in, the reality I was about to face. This culminated in intense stress and intense pressure. I felt I had to figure it all out and solve each problem I was encountering.

Little did I know at the time, but alcohol was quickly becoming my solution to emotional turmoil and internal conflict. The few nights a week of a couple of beers turned into most, if not every night of the week, of having several beers. It was such a quick "fix" for the whirlwind of bullshit in my head. My itch for distractions and partying was growing stronger – and my need to escape what sober life contained was immense. How on earth could I deal with everything going on in my head? Everywhere I turned, something stood out to me that reminded me of how different I was, how lost, confused, and hurting I was each and every day.

Alcohol was my reprieve, my solution, my only real friend. It temporarily silenced the chaos within me. Each sip seemed to drown out the relentless thoughts and overwhelming emotions that haunted my mind. It became a ritual, a crutch I leaned on to navigate through the maze of my thoughts. However, the more I relied on it, the more tangled and distorted my emotions became. I didn't know how to manage my emotions or how to calm myself. All this internal questioning put me in a state of mind where I believed everyone else was right and I was wrong. My negative voice was loud and strong. I needed something external to validate what I was doing, saying, or feeling to be "normal" and feel OK or accepted. I needed to feel like my life was OK and that other people were just like me.

A part of me knew I was unique and talented, but most of me didn't believe it and sure as hell wasn't going to show it – that would only make me more distant from society. It seemed like the world had a set standard for what was considered "normal," and I desperately wanted to fit into that mold. The fear of being seen as different or standing out held me back from fully embracing my abilities.

I constantly sought external validation, whether it was through the approval of others, societal norms, or even comparing myself to those around me. I believed that if I could just conform to what was deemed acceptable, then maybe I would finally feel like I belonged.

But deep down, there was a nagging voice reminding me that conforming wasn't the path to fulfillment. It whispered the importance of authenticity and self-expression. It reminded me that true happiness could only be found by embracing my uniqueness rather than suppressing it. I was too afraid, however, to accept myself for who I was and be myself in the world. My social anxiety was growing fast, and I had no idea that my behaviors and thoughts were only reinforcing the disorder. I believed pretty much everything my negative voice would tell me. Those thoughts grew strong enough to solidify as true beliefs about myself.

By June 2011, my home had become an awkward, uncomfortable, and tense environment. The signs of discontent were palpable, and the realization that my wife and I were both mired in unhappiness loomed heavily. In the midst of this turmoil, my wife, seeking solace and a breath of fresh air, took a role as a helper at the daycare attended by our son. It was a decision that would unravel the fabric of our family life.

By the end of June, the fractures in our relationship had deepened, leading my wife to make a pivotal decision. She left, seeking refuge with newfound friends for a few weeks. In her absence, I found myself navigating the challenges of solo parenthood, an endeavor that induced panic attacks at the mere thought of managing this life on my own, especially when it came to being a supportive and present parent.

Shortly thereafter, on July 10th, I received a text message from her, short and sweet, saying she wanted a divorce. I was at my mom's house at the time with my son, and I was breaking down in heartbreak and stress. All of this insanity had been going on for so long that just living my life felt like a war. I had begged her to talk to me, but she said she couldn't because she was busy swimming with her friends. I was crushed, to say the least. The betrayal, the lies, the realization I was only being used until a "better" option was available. This moment, and the months to come, changed me. It changed me in ways that, to this day, I'm still trying to understand the full reach of the scar.

I had to cut my life in half. And I did it fast. Within a week of that message, I had split everything, including the couch, in half. All bank accounts, retirement, beneficiaries, shared accounts, cell phones, cars, everything was split. I had a moving truck there within a few days, and while she was out partying with her friends, I packed up my half and moved back to Oxford. I rented a townhouse in the neighborhood I grew up in. It was the only place I knew to go, and I felt relatively "at home" in that neighborhood.

I rebuilt my life there. It felt like starting from the beginning but with a little more life experience. Describing the feeling of living there is still a challenge – it was an ambivalent mixture. There was a new sense of freedom, autonomy, and optimism, all contrasted with grief, sadness, and fear. Despite the annoying mixture of emotions, my townhouse quickly felt like home, a safe place. I could escape the world there. I was in control of every aspect of my life, and with the liberation from a debilitating marriage, I literally felt lighter on my feet.

After establishing the basics and laying a foundation for my son and me, I needed to sort out the finances. Luckily, at the time, I was using the GI Bill for school, which paid me a monthly housing allowance. I subsidized the rest of our living expenses through loans and working my butt off. I got a job as a cook at the old restaurant I worked at in high school and picked up where I left off six years prior. My routine became school during the day, time with my son mid-afternoon, and work at night. Rinse, and repeat for five and a half years.

Within a month, I had started to make friends, initially based around drinking, drugs, and partying, but nevertheless I was able to socialize. I started hanging out with the older college students who worked at the restaurant, alongside some of my old friends who worked there as well. Being a college town, there was always something going on at night. Oxford is riddled with bars, party houses, hangouts, etc., which meant every night was a party.

At the restaurant, when it became time to close, one of us cooks grabbed a case of beer from the gas station across the street. We started drinking while we cleaned up in preparation for going out shortly after we finished. Everyone would go home, clean themselves up, and head out for the night. A lot of times, we would meet at my house or one of our friends' places before heading to the bars. There was no telling what these nights would lead to. Sometimes, it was a few drinks and talking with people; other nights, it was party drugs all night. Nevertheless, I craved that atmosphere more than daylight. The chemical-induced euphoria took me away from everything in reality, and I could be in the present – completely detached from the burden that became living.

My new routine was challenging but nevertheless one I kept going for years. When I first moved back to Oxford, my wife and I would alternate weeks with my son. The weeks I didn't have him would be spent drinking, doing drugs, and school. I missed him and the tiny family I was doing my best to build. Ironically, the weeks I had him were emotionally defeating. There was no partying at night when he stayed with me and no self-medicating to escape.

My son was a visual reminder of the weaknesses I felt and the shortcomings I believed to have as a person and as a father. I felt inept, inadequate, scared, and lost. I was ashamed of myself for feeling so ill prepared for where I was in life. How could I be so behind the curve? My mind would take a deep dive into some debilitating realms of negative self-talk, which worked like a vacuum - bringing with it more self-doubt, insecurity, and embarrassment. My anxieties grew and grew until they controlled me. I was a slave to my anxiety's commands. It told me whether or not I could attend a class that day, if I could manage to grocery shop without having an anxiety attack, and if I should start drinking before work.

Before long, alcohol was the prerequisite for doing almost anything outside of my house. I used it to drive out the fearful thoughts and allow me to take care of my responsibilities. I dealt with the ambivalence of having to drink to feign happiness because at least I could fake it long enough to interact with people and feel somewhat a part of society. It was just easier to ignore my negative thoughts when I drank. What I didn't realize was I was letting my depression and anxiety go untreated, unaddressed, and unacknowledged. My avoidance behaviors and my belief in the negative self-talk were just reinforcing the problem itself.

My desire to drink became more and more frequent; I'd have a couple of drinks at lunch to ease the itch before I was able to have more in the evening. A continuous rotation between the worlds of sobriety and intoxication that controlled my life. During the brief moments of clarity, the nights alone, and the lonely days, I knew there was something I needed to do about my mental health. This lifestyle wasn't healthy and definitely not sustainable. I wasn't addressing anything at hand; I was only finding ways to drown it out. After months on a repeat of the same cycle, those problems, irrational thoughts, and the beliefs I had were still there. It was time to do something about it.

For me, social anxiety began in high school. I didn't think much of it; I thought it was part of the process of growing up. However, instead of ignoring and debunking my negative voice over the years, I listened to it instead. I had believed what it was telling me – when, in reality, it was a bunch of irrational nonsense. In doing so, I was laying the groundwork for a social anxiety disorder to run amuck. Fast-forward to my early 20s, and that's exactly what it did.

I started looking into what I was experiencing, trying to learn more about myself and life in general. I was googling everything I could think of related to the feelings I had. Eventually, I came across some therapy methods that I could do on my own from the comfort of my house. I found a program that was roughly 23 weeks long, each week being a different focal point built off of the previous week. It was cognitive-behavioral therapy for social anxiety.

Each week, I would listen to a session, complete some worksheets, and do the associated exercises. I treated that program like I had found a pot of gold, and truthfully, I did. I listened to every word and had journals and notebooks filled with notes and rationalizations about my thought process. I was understanding the full reach of the issue and how much of my life was impacted by this problem, and I was learning ways to truly address it. This marked a turning point for me as I took responsibility for my own contentment. I took ownership of the effort required to make things better. It was hard work, something that I maintained doing for years to come.

I had hoped the therapy was a relatively quick solution. What I didn't realize is that changing your thought process, and especially your beliefs, is a slow, steady, and gradual process. By the time I started this therapy, I was deep into the problem. Without a doubt, I had let these things go on for far too long. I wasn't exactly crawling in free time, either. I was still under the gun with school, kids, and work, so finding time to reflect and practice was challenging. By this point in my life, my head would spin like a carousel of flashing images of me failing and losing, being lost and scared, and being alone. I'd eventually break down, unable to handle it anymore, and cry, wishing someone understood this and could help me.

Everything in the world felt new, but I was in a stage of life where I thought I should have had more knowledge and experience. This conflict kept me hiding my true self, putting on a front to the world that I had it all together. Until I ultimately couldn't anymore. The beginning of May 2014 was my breaking point. Up until then, I was having daily anxiety attacks. My mind was always racing, and I didn't know how to slow it down. I would get home from my internship completely exhausted, barely able to speak and form sentences. All I had to look forward to was the relief I would get from drinking as soon as I walked in the door.

My life just wasn't sustainable this way. I knew something was wrong, and I needed help with my mental health. I had let this go untreated for years. How could I ever turn it around? I ended up resigning from my internship - there was no way I could make it through the summer term, keeping my situation under control. I felt like I lost the battle. Too weak and scared to hack it in society, I suppose.

Luckily, I was able to move back into my mom's house and into my old room. I packed up my whole house and put it in storage, unsure of when I would be able to get it back out. The last night that I had my townhouse, I slept on the living room floor under some cardboard. I was so embarrassed and sad to have given up my independence. How in the world was this happening to me? Am I really this broken after feeling that I was doing great just years prior? I spent the next couple of months essentially doing nothing but watching Netflix in my room. I wasn't working, school didn't start until the fall, and my son was with his mom for the summer. I didn't have the mental drive to do anything. I would lay on my bed all day, drinking beers and thinking endlessly, staring off at the ceiling. Days and nights blurred, my sleep schedule was non-existent, and a routine was merely a thing of the past.

As the summer went on, I began to think about what my next steps may be. I couldn't just lay in bed forever, doing nothing all day but sulking. I at least needed to pick up a job and figure out what to do about school before it started up in the fall. I only had two semesters left until I would reach my goal of graduating with a chemical engineering degree. I at least needed to reach that point, then I could figure out what in the world I would do next. I decided to continue school that fall semester and got a job at another kitchen in uptown, Oxford.

Starting the job was a great decision. It got me out of my funk, out of my head, and back to being around people. I met new friends over time and started hanging out again. I ended up getting involved with a server at the restaurant; she was always out with us and our group of friends. I was in no place mentally to entertain a relationship, but it brought a sense of connection and gave me someone to confide in. She drank a lot, too, and liked to go out. She was finishing up college at the same time I was, which worked out in our favor. As we both approached graduation, we wrestled with what we would do next. She originally planned on moving back to Columbus, and I was still living at my mom's house. Not exactly the greatest arrangement. With no career path laid out for me, I had no clue how I would get my own place again and be on my own two feet.

Shortly before graduation, I was approached by the company I interned with about starting a full-time position there. This came as a surprise for many reasons, especially since I figured I would take even more time off that summer. After some contemplation, I took the job and started forming a plan for myself. I had a girlfriend and a job and now needed my own place again. Despite my apprehension and fear, I decided to move out and get another townhouse on my own. Instead of moving back to Columbus, my girlfriend decided to live with me, which was a massive mental relief. I wasn't alone; I had a friend to talk to, someone to share my time with, and someone I could confide in.

Life began to stabilize, and we fell into a routine. A prominent component of that new routine was drinking. Each night after work started with hard liquor until we were drunk enough to ignore the real world. We never really did anything out of the house during the week; we were homebodies who liked to drink. The weekends included hanging out with our friends who still lived in town, having BBQs, and drinking all day.

Some people started to leave and start their real lives after college, and others stayed behind doing the same old thing. Seeing people move on provoked some challenging thoughts and emotions. How could these people feel so comfortable taking the next step?

I felt safe and steady in my routine, away from change and the unknown. I didn't feel secure enough in my own being to do anything new. I was somehow able to muster up the courage to be on my own again - how could I move away from this haven and rely on myself even more? I had just had a mental breakdown - what if that happens again? To calm these pesterous thoughts, I turned to my medication of choice and solidified my reliance on alcohol even further.

Gradually, I was beginning to feel my anxiety strengthen again. Going to work took all of my will and strength. I felt like an imposter there, hiding my internal struggles as best I could while trying to grow professionally and be a reliable resource. It was draining every ounce of energy I had. All of the hiding built walls between me and everyone else. It's impossible to connect with people and find common ground when you're muffling your own voice. Each day was chipping away at me until I decided to do something about it before I broke down again. So, one day at lunch, I drove myself to the VA hospital ER to ask for help.

I started seeing a therapist there and started taking medication for depression and anxiety. Seeing the therapist was truthfully very helpful. I became more comfortable and was able to be vulnerable and honest about the embarrassing thoughts I would have. The therapist helped me rationalize a lot and would point out things I wasn't able to see. It was a confidence booster just knowing I had him in my corner for support and knowing I could ask him the questions I tried to answer on my own. Those sessions gave me something to look forward to. Not only could I learn something, but I got to talk to another human as my true self, with no censorship and shame.

By the following summer, I had figured out a plan to move closer to the city, and my girlfriend and I took the leap. We got an apartment just 10 minutes from the city and settled in. It was an exciting time. We brought along with us our drunken, carefree lifestyle and love for partying. Life continued much like it was in Oxford. We drank heavily every night and did benders on the weekends. We cooked a lot of good food and would invite whoever we could over to join our impromptu parties. We were consuming about a liter of liquor per night during the weekdays and multiple bottles per day over the weekend. Needless to say, Mondays were rough. It was only on Wednesday that I felt relatively normal. Just for me to repeat the cycle again come Friday night.

As time went on, I was becoming more aware of my reliance on alcohol to maintain the life I had created, including my relationship with my girlfriend. She and I rarely had any time together in a sober state - our entire relationship was founded in a drunken state with drunken thoughts and drunken emotions. There was always an odd dynamic between us until the drinks started flowing. We both were different people with different values when we were intoxicated.

Life was becoming mundane, and being sober meant dealing with reality, so I needed a distraction, something to look forward to. My girlfriend and I started looking into building a new house. I had some friends and coworkers who had done it, and it seemed like an exciting experience. We decided to have a house built out in the country in a new development. This became my project and something to occupy my mind with. It gave me a future state to focus on and something to work towards that didn't involve my own self.

Chapter 6: Part 3 – Career and Collapse

"I must be willing to give up what I am in order to become what I will be."

-Einstein.

In December 2017, I started a new chapter of my life—as the proud owner of a house with a backyard to call my own. It was a milestone, a tangible symbol of my hard work and determination. Owning a house was something new for me. It came with a bunch of different feelings because now, I had this whole place to take care of. When I walked into my new home, it felt amazing because it was a goal I had wanted to accomplish for a long time.

The sense of pride was not only rooted in the tangible bricks and mortar but also in the intangible achievements that accompanied this new phase of life. Simultaneously, excelling at my job added another layer of fulfillment, reinforcing the feeling that I was indeed on the right path. Everything seemed to be falling into place, a testament to the choices I had made and the efforts I had invested.

However, our drinking continued and was gradually increasing in quantity. After a while, we both started to notice that our lives were simply work and drink, week in and week out. My sober state at this time was something I had wished to only have to experience a few hours a day. All the things about me and my mental health flooded me when I was sober. It was too much to process, let alone attempt to organize.

My drinking began to show its negative side as my relationships with my children were being hindered, my growth as a person, parent, and professional were essentially paused, and I was experiencing withdrawal symptoms when too much time had passed before I drank. By the end of the workday, my pupils were dilated, my hands were shaky, and I couldn't focus. Sometimes, I would stop at the bar just down the street for a couple of drinks before making the 35-minute drive home.

I wasn't just psychologically addicted to alcohol; I realized I was physically dependent. In May 2018, I decided I needed to make a change and either stop drinking altogether or drastically cut back. I saw my Dr and was prescribed medicine to safely come off of the daily drinking. With that, I started thinking about what my future would be like without alcohol. A lot of strain was placed on my relationship with my girlfriend because she also wanted to cut back but struggled as well.

The mutual soberness led us to part ways in December of 2018, and our 5-year long drunken abyss came to an end. I thought to myself that my drinking would go down and I could focus on developing myself and growing. However, I underestimated how much living alone would affect me. Living in the house I built for a long-term relationship that ended relatively abruptly and coming home to just myself and the cats tugged on my sadness and brought my depression to the surface with ease.

My plans of stopping drinking proved futile, and I continued to drink, always finding an excuse to do so. Just a few days after Christmas 2019, I checked myself into a detox center - the drinking had been going on heavily for far too long, and I needed to stop safely and hopefully get some professional guidance. After detox, I stayed sober for roughly a month, then convinced myself I had control again. I started having drinks, and just over a month later, I was back in detox. Missing work was putting additional strain on my career, and now my drinking was impacting my livelihood. I was still early in my career with a small professional network - losing my job would have been financially catastrophic for me.

Again, I stayed sober for just over a month before drinking again. Thankfully, I saw the cycle happening and stopped it before I needed an in-patient detox. I went to the ER and was treated and given medicine to detox at home. During the sober periods of this cycle, I became involved with a woman who I was truly infatuated with, someone I saw a future and family with. I knew after my trip to the ER that my drinking needed to stop altogether, or I would lose her and everything along with it.

The frequent spiraling into detox and/or the emergency room was enough to convince me that I had a serious issue with alcohol and needed to not only stay away from it but learn to live without it altogether. Much to my dismay, I started this journey beginning with that ER visit. Surprisingly, it went well, and I remained sober for roughly 13 months. Granted, I was motivated by nurturing my newfound love and also the internal voice telling me it was time to move forward, time to leave the party behind.

This meant experiencing things in a new light and a new perspective. This was admittedly challenging. Experiencing what most people experience daily felt new to me. Some days were overwhelming, frustrating, and too much to deal with. Sometimes, I would come home from work and just lay down for a power nap to unwind and be away from people, so I wouldn't say things out of annoyance or personal struggle. I did what I could to remain patient with myself and take things slow, allowing myself to learn and grow.

Occasionally, the thought of drinking would cross my mind like an involuntary reflex. I didn't always know what prompted the thoughts of drinking, whether it was a smell, a scenario, or a feeling. I couldn't pin it down. However, each time that happened, I made a conscious thought to dismiss the craving and focus on what was happening directly around me. This was a useful technique for me at the time. The craving quickly subsided, and I went about my business.

For 13 months, I steadily made progress in learning to live sober and manage myself and life without substances. As time went on, the effort I was putting into a sober mindset was decreasing. I naturally began to think I had reached my goal, regained control of myself, and could continue on without a deliberate effort to develop myself and reinforce a sober perspective. This was ultimately my addiction, slowly taking back control in a subtle, quiet, gradual way.

In the beginning of the summer, a friend of mine and a previous coworker from out of town was back in the area and wanted to hang out. I was initially excited until my anxiety ramped up. I hadn't really hung out with people in my natural sober state since I began my journey. I'm innately an introvert and inwardly focused. Socializing typically takes additional effort on my behalf. Hence, I would always associate drinking with socializing. I became nervous, which is an odd response to hanging out with a friend. But I felt like a different person when I drank, and I told myself that people wouldn't like or accept my sober state.

With all of this in mind, coupled with my length of sobriety and decreased work in remaining sober, I felt as if it would be safe to have a couple of beers with an old friend. This event marked the beginning of a two-year roller coaster of relapses, with each occurrence worse than the last. Having those drinks awakened a craving for alcohol I hadn't really had over the past 13 months. It was a strong desire to be back in my old mentality, my old alter-ego, that came with my intoxication.

I quickly fell back into old habits, having drinks after work, drinking on the weekends, or to help a hangover. The frequency spiked, and then so did the quantity. I felt guilty about my desire to drink as much as I did, especially about the amount I wanted. I would hide drinks and lie about the amount I had to make things seem less severe. It didn't take long until I started on benders, unable to resist the urge for more. Every thought was consumed by when and how I would get my next drink and how I could sustain drinking consistently. I wasn't thinking about work, my house, my family, my health, or anything of importance. Responsibility went by the wayside until I knew I had more alcohol to continue forward.

This vicious cycle of relapse and detox continued as I struggled to let go of that craving. My addiction would consume my mind and find clever ways to convince me it was ok to drink despite my life falling apart every time I did. Why would I trust something that always lied to me and always led me to despair? If I decided not to trust it, how do I make it stop? I eventually gave up and accepted that for me to get better, for me to become internally alleviated from this crutch, I needed to accept all of the things I've been trying to hide and push away. All of the anxieties and depression, resentments, anger, and sadness would need to be felt; it would need to be acknowledged, experienced, and processed. This meant struggle and hardship. I felt as if I was defeated. However, this is ironically a victory. Besides, what's worse – going through the turmoil of emotions I've tried to bury or free-falling deeper into an addiction to the point of drinking myself to death? Do I want to die or want to live a better life? I chose a better life, and I chose the hard path because the hard path leads me to awakening, peace, and contentment.

Chapter 7: Reborn Through Reflection

"As long as you live, keep learning how to live."

-Seneca.

If only stopping addiction were like flipping a light switch. I wish it was. My process has been more like a sound wave, and I believe it's like that for many. As mentioned earlier, addictions can form by various mechanisms; however, the initial outreach to drugs and alcohol to mask emotional turmoil may be a top contributor. People can easily find solace (temporarily) in the use of drugs and alcohol – that's obvious – but when appropriate methods to address inner distress aren't implemented and the use continues, an addiction is growing and growing.

I've heard more techniques on thought stoppage, avoiding triggers, relapse prevention, etc., than I can even count. The problem with these things is they are addressing the current addiction and not the original cause of it to begin with. Think of it like a candle, and the flame is the addiction. The wick of the candle is you, and the wax contains your inner struggles, emotional pain, trauma, and grief. Now, think of the techniques I just mentioned – all of those are ways to try to reduce the size of the flame, but they could never put out the candle entirely. Before the wick completely burns away, why not try to remove the wax instead?

In my profession and many others, this sort of methodology is referred to as root-cause analysis. Essentially, you have an undesired outcome or event that you need to prevent from happening in the future. Therefore, you must break down the process and investigate potential failure modes of that process. In our case, the undesired outcome is addiction – but what was the process or processes that played a part in the formation of that addiction? And how did those come about? What can be done to prevent the failure mode from happening again? In the case of the candle, we need to remove the wax.

To irradicate the fuel of an addiction, a pinnacle and necessary starting point is self-reflection. Our minds give us this capability, which can be rudimentary in cognitive and behavioral changes when used properly. Definitively, self-reflection is the capacity and willingness to witness and evaluate our own cognitive, emotional, and behavioral processes. This is no easy task and will take time and patience. It is a practice, not a task.

How do we self-reflect? To gain a deeper understanding of ourselves, we take the time to ask ourselves questions about our feelings and why we experienced them. We're learning a new level of ourselves and how we process the outside and inside world. A simple way to start is to ask yourself, "Why?" And once you find your first answer, ask yourself, "Why?" about that. Repeat this until you find yourself at a point where you can't get a much simpler answer. Be honest, be vulnerable, and be truthful.

We're looking for thought processes and thought sequences that lead us to undesirable emotions, which then add fuel to our addictions. We're hunting, finding the reasons – big or small – that cause us affliction. And by doing so, we can then begin to implement solutions that are healthy, positive, and effective. Keeping a simple notebook or journal of this is a great way to keep track of these thought processes. Take one page, write the outcome at the top, then each time you ask "Why?" write the answer below. When you've reached your final answer, you can then write out some possible solutions. Doing this activity alongside the guidance of a therapist will help to identify a common denominator in some situations and ways to address it. Some solutions may be obvious, while others may be a bit more complex.

Let's evaluate some benefits of this practice. Self-reflection is essential for personal growth and development as it allows individuals to deeply understand themselves, their thoughts, emotions, and actions. Here are some key reasons why self-reflection is important:

1. **Self-awareness:** Self-reflection enables you to gain a deeper understanding of who you are, your values, beliefs, strengths, weaknesses, and goals. It helps you identify patterns and behaviors that may be hindering your personal growth, enabling you to make conscious choices for self-improvement.

2. **Decision-making:** When you take the time to reflect on your experiences and choices, you can evaluate their outcomes and assess whether they align with your desired outcomes and values. This self-awareness helps you make better decisions, improving your personal and professional life.

3. **Learning from mistakes:** Through self-reflection, you can recognize your mistakes, take responsibility for them, and learn from them. This process helps you grow and avoid repeating the same errors in the future, fostering personal development and growth.

4. **Setting goals:** Self-reflection supports the process of setting personal goals by helping you clarify what is truly important to you. By reflecting on your values, aspirations, and priorities, you can set meaningful goals that align with your authentic self.

5. **Emotional intelligence:** Self-reflection enhances emotional intelligence because it allows you to identify and understand your emotions better. By recognizing your emotional triggers and reactions, you can regulate and manage your emotions more effectively, improving your relationships, resilience, and overall well-being.

6. **Problem-solving and creativity:** Self-reflection stimulates critical thinking and creativity. When you take time to reflect on a problem or challenge, you can evaluate different perspectives, generate new ideas, and find innovative solutions. This enhances your problem-solving skills and promotes personal growth.

7. **Building resilience:** Self-reflection helps build resilience by encouraging you to focus on your strengths and past achievements. It reminds you of your ability to overcome challenges and bounce back from setbacks, enhancing your self-confidence and ability to navigate difficulties.

Spending time reflecting on ourselves can bring about some enlightenment on not only our actions but our thoughts. With that in mind, there are things we've done, things we've said, and surely things we regret. It's a wish to be better and different, at least for me, and fuel to that feeling is the embarrassment, shame, and guilt associated with the things I've done while under the influence. I carry with me the weight of these thoughts. They hold me back from forward growth; they cloud my sunny days. They separate me in half.

So, how do you let go of that? How do you rejoin your pieces and mend yourself back into the beautiful being that you actually are? Well, the answer is paradoxical. It begins with self-acceptance. This acceptance does not mean that we are accepting alcoholism, addiction, or accepting a negative perspective of ourselves. This is a rational, in-the-present inventory of who we are right now. We know we want to be something better, and we know the things we wish we didn't have to deal with. But the fact is, we are who we are right in this very moment, whether we like it or not. We have to draw the starting line. We have to stop wandering, center our compass, and let go of wishes and guilt. There's nothing we can do about what's already happened, but there is something we can do for what's going to happen.

When we look at ourselves, we think of our inner self like a toolshed. When you walk inside that toolshed, it's filled with all sorts of items, some shiny and some rusty. Some are brand new, some used but well taken care of. Some tools are broken but sitting by the front door of the shed because they're frequently used. What we need to do is walk into that toolshed and find the items that we no longer need, that have no value to us, and get rid of them. They're just taking up space. As we walk through the shed, we can find things we do want to hold onto and probably some brand-new tools that we've had this whole time but are still in the package. These tools are the characteristics that define us, the skills we choose to embody, and the person in which we present to the world. Throw out the trash. Make room for some new tools.

As we accept ourselves, we need to speak kindly to ourselves. Most importantly, we need to actually say it out loud. You need to hear it, and you need to say it. This makes a difference neurologically as well. On a daily basis, in private, remind yourself of who you are, how far you've come in this life, and how, regardless of your past, you are diligently working and striving towards a better you. We are not accepting our faults as permanent; we are accepting that right now, we have growth ahead of us.

Navigating this process is challenging but not impossible by any means. You must remember that breaking free from addiction, engrained behaviors, and habits is something that should not and cannot be done alone. You must confide in a loved one, a close friend, a therapist, or a counselor. Your inner voice will play games with you – you have multiple neural pathways firing simultaneously. Do not fall into the trap of trying to choose which voice to listen to alone – because the unfortunate truth is you will likely choose poorly.

As I went through this myself, my first step was accepting that I couldn't continue running away from my feelings. I needed to sit with them, understand them, and process them. It was like untangling a knot that had been tightening for years. As I began to unravel the threads of my emotions, I found that each layer revealed a deeper understanding of myself.

Acknowledging my anxieties was like shining a light on the shadows that had been haunting me. I could see them clearly, and by facing them head-on, their power over me began to diminish. It was scary, but with each step, I was reclaiming control over my life.

Depression was a heavy burden I carried, but facing it allowed me to explore the root causes. It wasn't just about feeling sad; it was about understanding why I felt that way. This self-discovery was painful yet essential for building a foundation for lasting change.

Resentments had built up like a wall around my heart. I had to break it down brick by brick, forgiving others and, perhaps more importantly, forgiving myself. Letting go of grudges was liberating, and it created space for compassion and understanding.

Anger was a powerful force that needed redirection. Instead of letting it control me, I learned to channel it into constructive actions. It became a catalyst for positive change, motivating me to address the issues that fueled my anger in the first place.

Sadness, too, needed its due. Grieving for the losses and disappointments in my life was a process of healing. It wasn't about wallowing in self-pity but acknowledging the pain and allowing myself to move forward.

The journey wasn't linear. There were setbacks, moments of doubt, and times when the emotional weight felt unbearable. But with each challenge, I reminded myself of the alternative—an existence overshadowed by addiction, leading to a potentially tragic end.

Choosing the hard path was, in essence, choosing self-love and self-preservation. It required immense courage to face the demons that had haunted me for so long. It meant saying no to the quick fix of alcohol and yes to the slow, sometimes painful, but ultimately transformative process of self-discovery.

As I navigated this challenging terrain, I began to notice subtle shifts. The intensity of my cravings lessened, and moments of clarity emerged. The hard path wasn't just about enduring pain; it was about uncovering the layers of my authentic self that had been buried beneath the numbing effects of addiction.

I started to appreciate the simple joys of life that had been drowned out by the noise of my struggles. Sunsets became more vivid, laughter more genuine, and connections with loved ones more meaningful.

The small victories—the days without a drink and moments of emotional clarity—added up to a sense of accomplishment and self-worth.

The hard path wasn't a one-time decision but a daily commitment to self-improvement. It required ongoing effort and resilience. There were days when the temptation to revert to old habits was strong, but the lessons learned on this journey fortified my resolve.

The path of recovery was messy, filled with setbacks and victories alike. There were moments when I had to dig deep, confront uncomfortable truths, and challenge the very core of my being. But with each challenge came growth, and with each step forward, I reclaimed a piece of myself.

Chapter 8: Remodel and Rewire

"I count him braver who overcomes his desires than him who conquers his enemies; for the hardest victory is over self."

-Aristotle.

As much as I wished, I just could not change overnight. I kept trying to, but it still didn't happen. I would wake up the same old me with the same old problems. Once I started my path through reflection, acceptance, and cognitive-behavioral therapy, I learned the immense value of patience. All I wanted was to change and be better, and I wanted to be better right now. But it just doesn't work that way. I had to learn to be patient with myself and patient with the process. Just as it took time for anxieties, depression, and addictions to form and strengthen, it will take time to resolve them as well. Don't let this discourage you; you will win as long as you continue to focus on ways to improve yourself. You will win as long as you are continuing the process of dismantling the unnecessary framework of addiction, anxiety, and depression.

There will be setbacks. However, we must remember that you can only have a setback if you've made progress. Sometimes, it's two steps forward and one step back. But that's still a step forward, and we need to focus on the forward progress we are making. Remind ourselves of the positive changes we're making, accept that there is still work to do, and accept that it takes time. We don't need to pressure ourselves to change faster. We don't want to use negative emotions to motivate these changes because that's only adding gas to a fire. We need to embrace a new mindset of enforcing a positive perspective on our situation. Accept where we're at right now, relieve any pressure, and focus on what you can do to improve instead of letting the negative voice in your mind pull you down.

We have to let the addiction-ridden neurons die away while we strengthen and create new neural pathways of sobriety and clarity. This is why the process will take time. Think of it like lifting weights in the gym. You don't get huge muscles overnight just because you want them. Getting angry that you worked out for a bit but still don't have giant biceps isn't going to help you. You're current mindset may want you to get angry about it or sad about it, but paradoxically, if you decide to shift your thought pattern to the fact that you've made a positive change of going to the gym, getting healthier, slowly growing those muscles, you will feel encouraged, happier, and even proud of yourself. Often, we are the last ones to see the changes in ourselves, but if you continue your efforts, those changes are happening whether you see them or not.

So then, how do we rewire our brains to a better version of who we are? How do we let go of the old ways of thinking? We take advantage of the fact that our thoughts and behaviors can rewire our brains over time. This is done through neuroplasticity, which means that our brains can change. And we can drive the change where we want it to go instead of letting the negative voice control our lives. It takes effort, and this is why it's important to be patient with not only yourself but the process overall.

To guide this process of changing our thought patterns and letting go of old ways of thinking, we turn to a method called cognitive-behavioral therapy, or CBT. It is a widely recognized and evidence-based therapeutic approach that focuses on identifying and modifying negative thoughts, emotions, and behaviors.

Cognitive Behavioral Therapy plays a crucial role in helping individuals recover from alcohol addiction and substance abuse. When it comes to alcoholism, CBT can address the underlying thoughts, emotions, and behaviors that contribute to the addiction. It helps you develop healthier coping strategies, identify triggers for drinking, and learn skills to resist cravings.

CBT sessions typically involve working with a therapist to explore your beliefs about alcohol, your triggers for drinking, and any negative thought patterns that may be perpetuating the addiction. Through various techniques, such as cognitive restructuring and behavioral experiments, CBT aims to challenge and modify these patterns to foster positive change.

Research has shown that CBT can be highly effective in treating alcohol addiction. It equips you with practical tools to manage cravings, handle stressors without resorting to drinking, and develop healthier habits. Moreover, CBT can also help address co-occurring mental health issues often associated with substance abuse. Many of us turn to alcohol as a way to self-medicate underlying anxiety, depression, or trauma. By addressing these issues alongside addiction treatment, CBT helps us achieve long-term recovery by targeting both the root causes of our substance abuse and the associated psychological factors.

We need to understand this process of change and understand what we're doing. The more information we have about managing the addiction as well as co-occurring anxiety or depression, the better. There is a well-known framework that describes how we as people go through processes of cognitive and behavioral changes that will help us understand what we're experiencing.

The change model of addiction and behavioral change is a framework used to understand and guide the process of making changes in addictive behaviors. One well-known model is called the "Stages of Change" model, also known as the Transtheoretical Model (TTM). It was originally developed by researchers Prochaska and DiClemente.

The Stages of Change model suggests that we go through a series of five stages when trying to make a behavioral change, such as overcoming addiction. These stages are:

1. **Precontemplation:** In this stage, the individual is not yet aware or doesn't acknowledge that their behavior is a problem and has no intention of changing.

2. **Contemplation:** In this stage, the individual recognizes their behavior as problematic and begins to consider making changes. However, they may still have mixed feelings and uncertainty about whether or not they are ready to take action.

3. **Preparation:** During this stage, the individual actively plans and prepares for change. They may gather information, set goals, and start taking

small steps toward making a change in their behavior.

4. **Action:** This stage involves the implementation of specific strategies and behaviors to modify the addictive behavior. The individual makes conscious efforts to change, often with the support of external resources, such as therapy, support groups, or medication.

5. **Maintenance:** Once the initial change has been made, the individual works to sustain and consolidate their new behavior. They develop strategies to prevent relapse and establish a sense of stability and longevity in their changed behavior.

It is important to note that these stages are not linear and can be cyclical, with individuals moving back and forth between stages. Relapse is also a common part of the process, and it does not mean failure. Instead, it is seen as a normal part of the change process, and the individual can learn from the experience and re-engage in the stages of change. As long as we keep our focus on making the change, we will win, and we will grow.

The maintenance stage is a very important stage. This is where we want to be and where we want to live. In order for that to happen, we will need to develop our own specific relapse prevention techniques. These will be unique to each person, which is why working with a therapist is a tremendous help in understanding yourself and how to continue your recovery.

Something that is unique to all of our addictions is a pattern that the Substance Abuse and Mental Health Services Administration (SAMSA) refers to as the thought-craving-use cycle.

The thought-craving-use cycle is a concept used to describe the pattern of addiction. It consists of three main stages:

1. **Thought:** The cycle begins with thoughts or triggers that prompt the individual to think about using the addictive substance or engaging in addictive behavior. These thoughts could be related to previous positive experiences, external cues such as seeing others using, or internal cues such as stress or negative emotions.

2. **Craving:** Once the thoughts of using or engaging in the addictive behavior arise, they can intensify into cravings. Cravings are strong desires or urges to satisfy the addiction. They can be both physical and psychological, often accompanied by a sense of restlessness and an intense need to obtain and use the substance or engage in the behavior.

3. **Use:** The final stage of the cycle involves acting on the cravings by using the substance or engaging in addictive behavior. The act of using provides temporary relief or pleasurable sensations, reinforcing the cycle and strengthening the association between the thoughts, cravings, and subsequent behavior.

We can take advantage of our knowledge of this cycle and catch ourselves when we start to see ourselves focusing on addictive thoughts. We can interrupt this cycle and stop it before the cravings increase and become stronger. Every time we notice ourselves starting this cycle, not only do we interrupt it and redirect ourselves, but we should try to remember what caused the thoughts to arise. Was there a certain place you were around? What emotions were you feeling? Was there a certain smell? Were you overworked, stressed, or lonely? By identifying these cues, we can piece together influences to our triggers and find ways to dissolve the association to addiction. Again, working through this with someone close to you, a loved one, or a therapist is paramount.

Our brains are powerful, but they're also flexible and moldable. As we remodel and rewire ourselves, we are bringing to the surface the best version of ourselves. It's a spring-cleaning of our neurons. Over time, the cravings, triggers, thoughts, dreams, and mental preoccupations will diminish. As we focus on CBT and reframing our thoughts to a positive perspective, the old negative neural systems weaken and dissipate. Remember that this is something that takes time. While you're changing, remind yourself to ignore the negative voice, ignore the cravings, because the negative voice is merely a liar. There is no point in trusting a liar. Trust the process of positive growth.

Chapter 9: Complacency Kills

"What man needs is not a tensionless state but rather the striving and struggling for some goal worthy of him."

-Viktor Frankl.

Life isn't easy, whether you're drinking or not. If anything, the drinking only makes it harder. Once we embark on our path to sobriety, we will still face challenges in life, and we will still have tough times. You can still get divorced when you're sober, you can still lose a job when you're sober, and you can still be in debt when you're sober. None of the above are reasons to resort to using again. As a matter of fact,there are zero reasons to use it again. If your mind is telling you that there is a reason – that's only an old thought pattern playing games with you, tricking you into falling back down. The less you listen to that voice, the weaker it becomes over time.

Recovering from addiction, addictive thought patterns, and addictive behaviors is an ongoing process. Initially, our focus is on the immediate changes in our lives related to addiction and alcoholism, like building a new daily routine, keeping yourself busy, and avoiding triggering people, places, and things. After that initial phase, our focus shifts into a continuous improvement mindset (at least it should). This is where we find ourselves in the maintenance stage of the change model, where we engage in behaviors and thought patterns to not only remain sober but to continue addressing any and all distorted thoughts, emotions, and behavioral patterns. It's personal growth. It's building ourselves up where we want to be.

In this arena, our enemy is complacency. Complacency can lead us to a false sense of security, making us believe we have completely overcome our addiction and no longer need to continue our self-reflection and continuous improvement. It leads us to think we can go back to our old ways of thinking and living and proceed on as usual. However, that's false. There is no "going back" to anything. Our compass now only aims north. It may sway east or west, but we don't let the compass point south in any direction because that's where we relapse.

Our recovery is continuous. It's as if we are walking up the downward escalator. As we continue to work on ourselves, we take steps upward. But if we become complacent, if we think we've beaten addiction and that we don't have anything to worry about, then we stand still on the escalator. We begin to slowly move downwards, closer and closer to relapse. This is the reality of our situation.

Staying aware of our need to remain consistent in our improvement is a critical aspect of remaining sober, especially for those of us who have struggled with alcohol because it is everywhere. It's on the front page of menus, it's on billboards, and it takes up 50% of gas stations and convenience stores. The marketing and advertising costs for alcohol are astonishing – over 9 Billion dollars spent annually to push alcohol down your throat. It's mind-boggling to think about that. When you see these advertisements, start asking yourself if they're realistic, and start paying attention to the bullshit that's out there just to keep you drinking that crap. I can relax on the beach without a beer or some ridiculous cocktail with an umbrella. I can go to a sporting event, business dinner, or hang out with actual friends without having to have alcohol. The people drinking it are probably using it for the same reasons we did.

I remember struggling with these types of situations and struggling with friendships when I became sober. When I told my "close friends" that I don't drink anymore, our "friendship" dissolved pretty quickly. I was hurt by this at first; I was upset and confused as to why I wouldn't hear from them anymore and why we didn't hang out until I realized that those "friendships" were just built around the use of some type of substance. There wasn't an actual connection there, and we weren't actually close; as a matter of fact, they barely knew the real me. To this day, I haven't heard from them, and quite frankly, it doesn't bother me at all. Why place value on something that doesn't return its worth? Why would I think the friendship is important when they evidently don't?

We have to learn to manage our expectations when we become sober. Friendships change, relationships change, and your own outlook on life changes. As we live a sober life, we will find new friendships that actually have value. Our connections with others in the world, whether friendly or romantic, will be more genuine because they're built around the real version of ourselves. We, as individuals, will find new things that we enjoy doing, new things we are good at, and new things we want to try. It's a new canvas for us, which, in reality, is something to be grateful for.

The concept of gratitude is tremendously helpful in our recovery and maintenance. It has immense benefits for our mental well-being, reducing cravings and keeping us on track. During times of depression or anxiety, or when we find ourselves going down addictive thought patterns and experiencing cravings, shifting our focus to what we are grateful for brings us into a more positive frame of thought and shuts down portions of the brain that cause us these negative emotions.

Feeling gratitude has a positive impact on the brain. Research has shown that when we experience and express gratitude, certain regions of the brain are activated. These regions include the prefrontal cortex, which is responsible for positive emotions, self-awareness, and decision-making, as well as the hypothalamus, which regulates stress.

When we feel gratitude, the brain increases the production of dopamine and serotonin, which are neurotransmitters associated with happiness and well-being. This can lead to an overall improvement in mood and a reduction in stress levels. Moreover, practicing gratitude regularly can strengthen the brain's neural pathways related to positive thinking and resilience. It can also help to counteract the brain's tendency to focus on negativity, as gratitude promotes a more optimistic and centered mindset.

Overall, feeling gratitude can lead to positive changes in the brain, including improved emotional well-being, increased resilience, and a greater sense of happiness and contentment.

Make a running list of things in your life that you are grateful for, and add to it as time goes on. Keep this list on a piece of paper, on your phone, in your wallet or purse. This list will be your tool against old thought patterns and behaviors. Gratitude is invaluable. When you feel like drinking or when you are feeling depressed or anxious, get your list out and go for a walk. While you're walking, read each line of the list slowly enough to remember the feeling that sentence gives you. Then move on to the next. Before you know it, not only have the cravings subsided, but you will be more focused on the present and less depressed or anxious. You are rewiring your brain, and you are continuing to improve. By doing this exercise, you strengthen your new neural pathways while weakening the old.

Chapter 10: Now What?

"Do not spoil what you have by desiring what you have not; remember that what you now have was once among the things you only hoped for."

-Epicurus.

I sincerely hope that through reading this book, you were able to take at least a tiny piece of information that may have been new to you and useful in some way. I'm hoping that in reading my story, you were able to resonate with a portion of it. I'm hoping you understand that if you're an addict/alcoholic and/or struggle with anxiety or depression, you are not alone. There are millions upon millions of us that struggle in silence. We walk past each other every day without even knowing it. We talk to each other while hiding the battle within us. What we need is to connect with each other and grow.

I think it goes without saying that the information provided in this book is merely the tip of the iceberg and by no means comprehensive. But these were some of the critical things that saved me from basically drinking myself to death. Looking back, it surprises me how I'm still above ground and able to write this book. I'm grateful to have the opportunity to at least try to help. I know that hearing others share their stories and the wisdom they've gained along the way has helped me tremendously, and I hope it does for you, too.

So now what? Where do you go from here? Well, if you've already started on your path to recovery, my advice is simple: keep on going and keep walking up the escalator. If you want to make a change, if you're tired of the habit but scared to let go, draw the line in the sand. Take a small but deliberate step in the right direction. Even if your support group is small or even nonexistent, there are several legitimate support avenues on social media and in person that I can attest to being helpful.

Keep yourself occupied. Goals, whether small or large, are important for self-worth and a sense of purpose. Set some small goals for yourself – they don't necessarily need to be related to addiction. Boredom is the face of relapse. You now have the opportunity to fill up the time you used to spend drinking, doing something you actually enjoy.

Work through and process your thoughts and emotions. Don't let them fester and go unaddressed any longer. Taking time to work on yourself and improve your quality of life is not a selfish act – you are getting healthier, and that is priority number 1.

You're embarking on a path towards a healthier and happier version of yourself and a healthier and happier life. Yes, change is scary at times and uncomfortable, so remember to take things slow, be patient with yourself, and as long as you keep your compass facing north, you will always be on the right path.

JEFFREY HOLLEY

The Parts of Me

In a world so vast, where thoughts unfurl,
Inside my mind, chaos and swirl,
Like fragments of a puzzle incomplete,
I'm six different people, yet I'm only me.

One voice speaks of courage and desire,
Another one fears, consumed with fire,
A dreamer dreams, forever chasing stars,
But reality holds back, it leaves its scars.

But as the days go by, and I search for peace,
I'll find a common ground and bring release,
I'll listen to each voice, I'll understand,
That all these parts of me, they make me grand.

I'll blend the dreamer and the skeptic's doubt,
The optimist and pessimist will find a route,
The warrior and worrier, hand in hand,
Together, they'll create an army to withstand.

So, as I navigate this intricate maze,
I'll embrace these facets in different ways,
In unity, I'll find strength and peace,
I'm the conductor of my mind's masterpiece.

9 7 9 8 8 6 9 2 7 6 6 3 6